CANT TURN BACK

A BOOK ALL ABOUT TRAVELLERS BY CHILDREN IN MOHILL, CO. LEITRIM

A new book by Kids' Own in partnership with The Arts Office, Leitrim County Council, Leitrim Partnership, Mohill Family Support Centre and The Department of Social and Family Affairs.

1

INTRODUCTION

Now that the Cant has started to come alive for my grandchildren and all Traveller's culture, I don't want to let it die. I was surprised that the children were so interested in it and now they ask me the whole time for words and what they mean. I tell them the Cant words and how I was reared up with the Cant. The Cant is only another way of talking like the Irish. I'd like to see more workshops about Cant not only in Leitrim but all over Ireland. I was very surprised to see how interested the settled children were in the Cant and all the questions they asked me. I was glad to be able to answer them. It was great to see Traveller children and settled children happy at the one thing. It's a big step to see the discrimination going away when they work together.

We have to find ways to bring the Cant to the schools, because it's good for the settled people not only Travellers to know what we are saying. Maybe the teachers and Traveller parents could support the children with the Cant in schools. It would be an awful thing to see the Cant going out, because it's like another part of education that we can all share. The beggin' days are gone but the Cant lingers on. Like our title says we Can't Turn Back to the old days but we can bring the Cant back.

Mary McDonagh

Welcome to our fabulous new book. We hope you enjoy it. Our book is all about the Cant language. Cant is the language Travellers spoke and lived long ago. Sixteen pupils from St. Manchan's primary school in Mohill and first year pupils in Marian College, Mohill made this book. Mary and Orla from Kids' Own and Mary Mc Donagh a Traveller from Mohill helped us in the workshops over eight weeks.

We made this book because the Cant language is dying out and we are trying to bring the language back. We put a lot of effort into making the book but we had fun as well. We hope you enjoy it.

UP MOHILL

Thanks to all our teachers and everyone who took part.

Michela Beck, Sharon Bohan, Laura Foley, Padraig Gallagher, Joshua Lynch, Mary Bridget McDonagh, Val McDonagh, Niamh McHugh, Ronan Miller, Oisin O'Driscoll, Claire Quinn, Niall Tiernan, Orlaith Cahill, Aileen Flynn, Caroline McDonagh, Bernadette McDonagh Shane McGowan, Martin McDonagh, Cait McHugh, David Mitchell, Patrick McDonagh, Pat McDonagh, Bernie McDonagh, Stephen McDonagh, Darren McDonagh, Frank Wall, Ordharnait McGuinness, Ethan Harkin, Celine Mulligan, Kate McCarthy, Tom Lavin, Mary Phair, Tina McLoughlin, and all at The Mohill Family Support Centre, Mary Branley, Orla Kenny and all at Kids' Own, Una Duffy, Bríd McMahon, Mary Scollen, and a special thank you to Mary McDonagh.

THANKS TO ALL OF US!

CONTENTS

KV-194-633

INTRODUCTION   PAGE 2

CONTENTS   PAGE 3

WHY DID CANT DISAPPEAR   PAGE 4

MAKING A CAMP   PAGE 10

MARRAIGE AND SLAGGING   PAGE 16

BEGGIN' AND GEIGIN'   PAGE 22

THE TRAVELLER WAY OF LIFE   PAGE 30

CURES   PAGE 44

GLOSSARY OF CANT WORDS   PAGE 46

HOW WE MADE THIS BOOK   PAGE 47

WHY DID CANT DISAPPEAR

HOW COME YOU STARTED SPEAKING ENGLISH?

Well, the Cant disappeared because when I reared my children I didn't learn it to them and they couldn't learn it to their children so that's how it went out. We didn't keep it up and at the time I had my children there was no begging for them. There was money coming in from the dole and it changed all the Cant.

It changed the beggin' and the halting sites, the houses changed the staying on the side of the road. That took away an awful lot of the Travellers' culture, that you couldn't stay where you wanted anymore, or make a camp where you wanted, or make a tent where you wanted.

From the 1970's it started going out because we didn't speak it to our children and that's how it went away like that. It's going away and our children and our children's children know nothing about it.

HOW WILL OUR BOOK HELP BRING THE CANT BACK?

Well, they can ask me questions, and they can read the book and they may start to talk it amongst themselves and try and bring it back if 'tis possible. I think it's going to be a hard thing, but I think the book will help them a lot and they can read it.

4

HOW CAN THE CHILDREN LEARN THE WORDS?

Well, that's why we're here trying to learn ye.

DID THE TRAVELLER PARENTS STOP SPEAKING THE CANT TO ONE ANOTHER?

No, the parents know the Cant, but the real old are gone and the likes of myself and my husband can still talk it or any one my age. But the children don't know it.

CLAUDÓG, CLAUDÓG, BOG ME A RUNÓG

HEN, HEN, GIVE ME A EGG

HOW DID THE LANGUAGE START OFF?

Well, that's going back a long, long way before I was born. It went on through the Travellers all the time, probably going back thousands of years. I learned it from my mother and she learned it from her mother and going all the way back. My Cant to me was the same as the Irish was. I don't know any Irish and if you were talking in front of me in Irish I wouldn't know what you were saying. Just like if I was talking the Cant, you wouldn't know what I was saying.

5

ARE TRAVELLERS THE ONLY ONES WHO CAN TALK THE CANT?

Yes. But ye're all learning it now.

MUGGLES - APPLES

LUSCÁN - FISH

WEED - TEA

DORA - BREAD

ALAMACH - MILK

CULLENS - SPUDS

INNOCKNIBS - TURNIPS

COB - CABBAGE

AID - BUTTER

FÉ - MEAT

GRITHUNS - ONIONS

DO SOME WORDS NOT HAVE A WORD IN CANT?

There's a lot of things that don't have Cant words, I'd say there's only a hundred and fifty left and if they go there'll be nothing left, and I have to thank ye for getting the children here so they can learn it, because it'll mean a lot to them in years to come.

THE CANT WORDS ARE HARD TO GET INTO YOUR HEAD, BUT IF YOU GO OVER THEM YOU'LL EVENTUALLY GET THEM.

My picture is a corraí pulling a wagon at night. Maybe the Travellers are moving to a different place. It was a tough way of life. I like this project, it is fun using the materials to make the pictures. The Cant words are hard to get into your head, but if you go over them you'll eventually get them. I hope our book helps us remember the Cant words.
Shane

THE MOST IMPORTANT THING IS THAT WE DON'T TREAT PEOPLE DIFFERENTLY!

My picture is about a Traveller fishing in a river, sitting on a rock. Fishing was a way to get food for the children and family. We shouldn't let the Cant die out because all the traditions and culture of the Travellers might go too. We have a chance to think about all the different things about culture. The most important thing is that we don't treat people differently and that the language won't go.
Cáit

I like learning the Cant because not many people know it. It's a good idea to tell other people about it so they can learn it. I didn't really know about Travellers in the old days.
Celine

9

MAKING A CAMP

We got wattles, or sticks from the woods, chimógs in the Cant, and we'd bend them so that they were round at the top and each end stuck in the ground. We'd get the mail bags and a calico cover, tarred to keep the rain out and we'd get straw or hay from the farmers and make a tick for the beds. The tent was called the lúbán and we made a lí inside for the goyas to sleep. We had another bigger camp for the fire the shelter tent, with the chimógs and nobera

In the morning me mother would get ready and she'd go out geigin the cénas. She had to tie the small childer inside the camp to the chimógs so they couldn't get out on the road. She'd geig for lúrp, weed, grucaire, gairead, and chercs for the goyas. Sometimes she got guilli-mies, nobera for the chera, skoi and alamach. Other times she might get a few rúmógs. Sometimes she salked the flowers for a few nucs. She made the flowers herself from crepe paper and wire stems.

CHIMÓGS – STICKS
LÚBÁN – TENT
LÍ – BED
GOYAS – CHILDREN
NOBERA – TURF
GEIGIN – BEGGING
CÉNAS – HOUSES
LÚRP – FLOUR
WEED – TEA
GRUCAIRE – SUGAR
GAIREAD – MONEY
CHERCS – CLOTHES
GUILLIMIES – SHOES
CHERA – FIRE
SKOI – WATER
ALAMACH – MILK
RÚMÓGS – EGGS
SALKED – SOLD
NUCS – PENNIES
MISSEL – GO/GET
STEAMERS – CIGS
GLEOCH – MAN
DORA – BREAD
CULLENS – SPUDS
CÚINNE – PRIEST
NOCAS – POTS

She'd missel back and bring home the steamers to the gleoch. We'd make the weed and bake the dora and boil the cullens. Me mother would put down the fé and the cob and the cullens in the big pot for the goyas and the gleoch. Next day she'd go into the grag for more geigin. She'd geig the cúinne and all the cénas in the grag. Sometimes she'd get nucs and more times she'd get a bit of dora. More times she might be told missel off. She had a candle for light.

The gleoch would make the nocas and buckets, and ponnies, hand gallons out of tin and galvanised. The beoirs would missel out salking. The beoirs used to swap anything like cans, or flowers or whatever they had for food, or whatever they needed. Sometimes we met with another family and we'd swap weed, steamers, or if we had nothing to swap we'd share. We made weed in a noca by boiling the skoi on the chera, and we'd put the weed and grucaire and alamach in the noca altogether and pass it to all the gleochs and beoirs.

My picture is the trailer, the shed with the turf and a tent. If I had a choice I would go back to the camping days, because it's a good way to live. Outside is a hard life if the weather is bad.

Bernie

My picture is about a camp in the rain. It has loads of hay, and turf. The hay is for making beds with sacks. The camp is brown because it is wood covered with material. Sometimes I'd like to live in a camp because it's big and you could keep the hay and the heat in it. If I had 20 brothers and sisters we would make 20 beds and pillows. It's a nice way to live but not in the rain or lightening or thunder. When the rain stops we will light a big fire with turf and sticks. Nobera is the cant word for turf and chimógs is the word for sticks.

Patrick

I made a camp for my picture, with the horse tied to the pole. Travellers like horses so much because in the olden times they had no cars and the horse pulled the wagons, a bit like you see on cowboy movies. My Dad likes cowboy movies, but they should be called horseboy movies.
Pat

My picture is about the inside of a caravan. There are two windows of different sizes. You have a small light and a big bed for all the children to sleep in. Some children sleep in bunk beds and the parents sleep on the sides. It's nice and warm sleeping in a trailer, you can hear lots of noise from outside, like thunder and lightening or rain. Sometimes if it's too hot outside in summer you go in the trailer for shade. If a parent has to go off the other parent minds the children.

When I grow up I want to have a house anywhere but hopefully in town maybe in Mohill. I'd like a house with stairs and a stove to keep you warm at night. I'd like four bedrooms. But if you were in a tent or a caravan and there were strong winds the tent and caravan would be knocked over or blown away, but the house would stay, because it's strong.
Martin

My picture is about Travellers camping on the side of the road. I think Travellers had a real hard life going out begging for food and camping. Their lives have changed an awful lot in the past years. I find it hard to understand some things about Traveller culture. Like why girls aren't allowed to talk to boys or why they leave school early and get married so young.
Michaela

MARRAIGE AND SLAGGING

Them days Travellers got married very young. The father of the súbla would ask the father of the lakín if a match was on and if the fathers agreed the marriage went off in a week. I was sixteen myself when I got married and today is my 37th anniversary.

SO YOU ARE GETTING THE HANG OF IT SO?

Well sometimes I felt like hanging myself. The Travellers always got married in a church, but I think 16 or even 18 is too young. They'd be better off waiting until they were 25 or 26 so they knew the world better, and didn't start a family.

WHAT DID TRAVELLERS WEAR TO THE WEDDING?

You just wore the clothes you were in and probably that afternoon you were off geigin' same as every other day. But the girl went with her family on the wedding night and the husband came to get her the next day.

DID ANYONE CAUSE TROUBLE FOR TRAVELLERS?

Well sometimes at night if the settled people or country people as we call them, were coming home from the pictures they might start slaggin' us, or throwing stones at the camp or try to pull the cover off the tent. We called that slaggin but nowadays it's called discrimination.

I made a wagon because the wagons were the most important thing for travelling around. Sometimes the mother and father slept in the wagon and they carried their stuff round in it. They used to travel with the wagon when they go begging. I'm finding out a lot of stuff that I didn't know about Travellers, like the language and how they lived. I'd like to go back in time to see how life was like for my Granny and parents. I imagine the tents would be cold at night and you'd have to go to the toilet behind the ditch.

The women had to clean up and mind the children while the men mended the buckets and fed the children and the horse. Traveller girls get married around 16 up, it's young but it happens. Girls leave school now at 16 and some girls and boys find school very hard. I find Irish hard. Traveller culture is different to settled people. In the settled culture people don't move a lot, they wait in one house for years or live on a farm. I hated going to school young because I was bullied for being a Traveller. I find it easy now because they know I can stand up for myself.

Being a Traveller girl like myself is sometimes good and sometimes bad. I can't have stuff like the other settled girls. I can't go out to discos. But a positive thing is moving out of your mother's house at a young age and you don't hide behind your parents, you stand on your own feet. Travellers always know when you are lying. If someone's says things about Traveller children the parents know if its lies or not. Traveller girls are not allowed to talk to boys by themselves at all. If they do, the girl will get in trouble with the mother or father. You might get grounded and have loads of work to do.

Mary Bridget

The Cant language is cool because it's not like Irish its different.

Sharon

I never knew that Travellers got married so young in the old days.

I have begun to understand more about Traveller culture since this project started. I didn't know about begging for food and clothes or that girls couldn't talk to boys.

The Cant language is cool because it's not like Irish it's different. I never knew that Travellers got married so young in the old days. I have begun to understand more about Traveller culture since this project started. I didn't know about begging for food and clothes or that girls couldn't talk to boys. Sharon

In the old days they didn't have weddings like we do now. They didn't dress up, they just wore normal clothes. They didn't have a reception either. Mary Bridget said the married couple didn't stay together the first night they got married, but the new husband came for his bride the next day. There were no presents either because Travellers had nothing to give each other. The newly married couple made their own camp from then on. Weddings were open invitation then and now, which means that anyone can come.

Nowadays Travellers have wedding dresses and suits and come to church in a limousine. They have big receptions but the same tradition exists where the husband comes for his wife the day after the wedding. Travellers getting married now are older than they used to be. There has been a lot of change for Travellers now that the begging days are over, the tinsmithing is over, and they don't move around all the time. They just move some of the time. I found it very interesting learning about Traveller culture.
Niamh

I came to Mohill in October 2007, a few months ago from South Africa I lived in a suburb close to a town called Benoni. It was a pretty basic town quite financial, banks and apartment buildings and one or two shopping malls. I came from quite an urban area mixed black and white. There is very little racism in that area now. Coming to Ireland is kind of refreshing because the people here are a lot more friendly and there's a lot more safety than in South Africa. It is different to have the majority here white. I have learnt that there are Travellers the world over. I found that the situation is similar to nomads in Southern Africa a few hundred years ago and the Irish Travellers of recent times. My picture is a Traveller boy of 15 or more who is away from his family at present.
Frank

Claire Quinn

My picture is a Traveller who works for all the farmers, making hay, doing the turf and driving a tractor, and anything else the farmer asked him to do. If the farmer had money he paid a few shillings to the Traveller, but if he didn't have money the farmer gave him food. My favourite part of this project was making the pictures for the book.

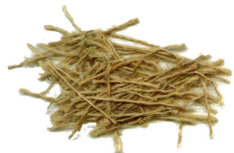

21

BEGGIN' AND GEIGIN'

YOU TALKED ABOUT GOING OUT GEIGIN' BUT WHAT WAS YOUR LIFE LIKE AS A LITTLE GIRL?

When I was a little girl, my life was just the same as my mother's. I had to go out and geig, go out the country with my mother and help feed the family and go to the farmers houses and beg for lurp, cullens, fé, weed and grucaire or anything you could get.

This picture is about Travellers hunting for rabbits. The gleoch has a snare made of wire. The other people in the picture are going out beggin'.

WHAT DID THE MEN DO WHEN THE WOMEN WENT OUT BEGGIN'?

Well, the men were still making the nucas, the ponnies and mending things, bottom buckets, kettles and pots for the farmers maybe for potatoes, turf or something like that. They'd take out the old bottom and put a new one in. Me father had a way of doing it with a hammer and stakes.

Joshua

23

My picture shows the mother and child begging from the farmer. Now no-one goes beggin' because they don't need to. I didn't know about Cant or any of the words before I did this project. The words are so different from Irish. It helps a lot to learn about their lifestyle in the past. My picture is of a farmhouse that the Traveller would have begged at.
Laura

This is an ordinary tent That we had in the old times.
In the old times we had to hunt for food.

25

My picture is about a family in the town in the old days. Three women are beggin' at the houses or as we say in Cant geigin' the grag for gaíread. The most interesting thing to me in the workshops was the storytelling about the Traveller way of life. I knew about the old days from my parents and grandparents but hearing the stories again with my friends from school was good. When I grow up and get married and have children I will teach the kids, Cant.

Bernadette

My picture shows the Travellers coming into the grag to geig. There's a cart and a woman holding a baby. I wouldn't like to go back to the old days because you didn't go to school much because you were travelling so much. So you wouldn't get an education. You need education to get a job, I'd like to be a teacher. The Traveller life style is changing, some things for the better, eg. you can have a stove in the house to keep warm and more rooms. We have a range in the hut and a stove in the trailer.
Caroline

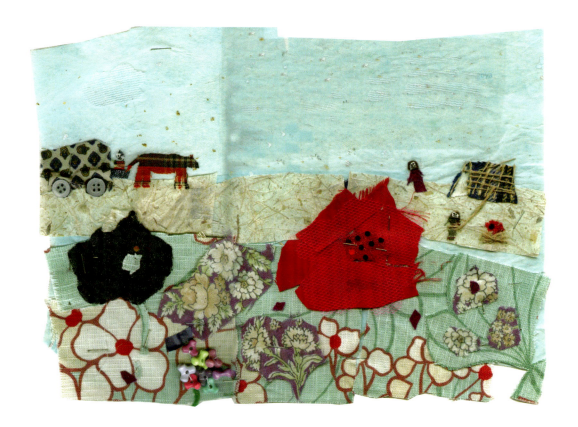

My picture is about Traveller life long ago. There is a
gleoch Travelling with his wagon to the camp. There
is a family at the camp, a beoir and a goya. The goya
is tied to the camp to stop her from going on the
road and getting run over. I think it was a hard life
but there were good things too. I never knew that
Travellers had their own language. The Language is
very interesting and i'm getting to learn new words,
Orlaith

My picture is about a Traveller family going through the grag in a horse and wagon. I put thatch on the houses and there's a beoir gegin the cénas I like learning the words because the language has nearly disappeared.

I like listening to the stories about the Travellers from the old days. I'd like other children to learn the words too so that we can speak the Cant and keep the language alive.

odharnait

29

THE TRAVELLER WAY OF LIFE

From tent to tent and house to house that's how they lived and that's what they done!

WHAT ABOUT GOING TO SCHOOL?

I didn't get much schooling 'cos my father moved round that often. I might be a day in school or two days in school, and the last school I was in was Gortlettra and that's a good many's years ago, and how I learned to pick up me reading, was from the newspaper and comics.

HOW DID YOU MAKE THAT OUT?

With the pictures I could follow the words and when I came to Mohill, to The Sisters of Mercy, Sister Micheal and Mother Stan and others helped me more.

WHERE DID YOU WORK?

I never worked in me life, until I came to Mohill and all me family is grown up. I started work nine years ago, September coming. I got a job with the Leitrim Partnership and it has changed me life in many ways and I'm more independent on myself for what I'm doing. From the tent to the house is a big change.

WHAT KIND OF PUNISHMENT DID YOU GET IF YOU DID SOMETHING BOLD?

Me father would get a sally rod in the woods and give a batin.

CAN YOU TELL US THE NAMES OF THE PLACES YOU MOVED ROUND?

The places we moved around were Mohill, Carrigallen, Gortlettra Ballinamore, Keash Carrigan, Arva, Drumshambo, Drumlish and Cappagh of the wires. The furthest me father ever went on the roads was Longford. Me father was originally from Donegal, a Letterkenny man and when he moved here he rarely moved out of Leitrim. His mother died at age 38 in childbirth so he was reared an orphan. He got married when he was eighteen and me mother was sixteen and they had twenty children, eighteen of them living.

WERE TRAVELLERS EVER FARMERS?

No, because if you're a farmer you have your own land and you stay in the one place. But Travellers don't own their own land so they move around trying to survive. The longest they ever stayed in one place was three weeks, a month at the tops. The Travelling way is nearly gone now, but still if Travellers are in houses they like to go and come back. T'was a very hard life the Travellers lived one time, the months from November to March very, very cold. We spent the winters in Cappagh of the wires maybe until February and then we go off out the country selling ponnies and looking for the horse hair. We'd sell it in Annaduff. We'd sell jam pots, Guinness bottles back to the shops anything bits of scrap anything we'd get a few pennies for. They call it recycling now. In them times it was the old money, the real old hen pennies and you don't get now. Maybe you never seen them. But it was long ago.

WHAT KIND OF CLOTHES DID YOU WEAR?

Anything the farmers gave us. And me mother used to wear a shawl. They call them car rugs today.

WHAT DID YOU EAT?

Anything the farmers gave us, and anything that kept us full and warm. And me father used to catch rabbits and hares.

DID HE SHOOT THEM?

The Travellers didn't have guns them times, me father used to make snares out of wires to catch the hares.

WHAT ABOUT FISHING? DID YOUR FATHER GO FISHING?

He did, for pike and eels in the lakes.

DID YOU HAVE FRIENDS IN SCHOOL?

We did but we weren't there very often. So there was a lot of slaggin' calling you tinker or not talking to you at all.

WERE THE FARMERS ALWAYS KIND OR WOULD SOME OF THEM BE BAD TO YOU?

Only for the farmers we wouldn't have survived as long as we did. Mostly they'd be kind but more of them would tell you missel off that means get away from around the house. My mother would look for anything she could get. She'd bring a side pocket with her so she could keep a few steamers, or pennies in it, a needle and thread, that was their safe. They had no handbags, or wallets.

IS IT A DIFFERENT LIFE FOR THE TRAVELLERS IN THE HOUSES?

It's a different life for the Travellers in the houses, even when the halting site started with the caravans and the huts. Now with the houses it's twice the life. My mother will be eighty soon and she's only in a house this two years, she never had a house before.

HOW IS SHE FINDING IT?

She found it strange at first but now like at her age, it's grand because it's warm and it's comfortable and someone comes there to look after her and all that. But she reared a family of twenty on the side of the road and from camp to camp and from town to town. Some days the children went hungry and more days they had enough.

WOULD YOU LIKE TO GO BACK TO HOW IT WAS?

Well I wouldn't like to, but even where I am now life has changed. But I'd like to see a lot of the old culture coming back, like keeping up the Cant. There are no Travellers on the side of the road.

DO YOU MISS IT?

Well indeed I did, I missed a lot of it, and I travelled a lot but it's just part of life, everything changes, and sometimes you wouldn't know if it was better or worse. But travelling is still in the blood the whole time.

WOULD YOU HAVE GOT JOBS BACK THEN?

The only jobs you got back then, was maybe the young fellas filling tractors of turf for the farmer, or bringing the hay in for them. They'd get a few shillings then if the farmer could pay them or they'd get food and turf from him.

32

HOW ABOUT NOWADAYS, DO TRAVELLERS GET JOBS?

Some of them are getting Fás schemes and getting great training. One time the Travellers wouldn't know about it, but it's out there now. The great thing now is that a lot of them is working.

The younger generation including my own family, they wouldn't know how to make a can or bucket. They never took it up after my father died. They know nothing about that. Only one man kept it up, that was Michael Lawrence in Longford, he used to make copper buckets and pots. And there was Tom Ward in Charlestown. But that's the only ones. Michael Lawrence is deceased now for a couple of year. So there's none of it going on at all. But

there's not much farming going on now either. Half the country is empty now, more people moved away into the towns and more of them deceased. There's hardly nobody in the country now so we could not live on the handouts. But we get the dole now and training and work schemes and all. Martin has two brothers in America working, one in Massachusetts and he's married this six years and working in a bank. I don't know where the other fella is. But his parents know because they keep in contact with him the whole time.

My picture is about the places Travellers moved in Leitrim. I never knew about the Cant before this. Our project is important because it will help promote the Traveller language and if Travellers want to keep it going they have to help too like Mary is doing. I hope in the future that Traveller culture keeps going and that settled people realise how lucky they are.
Padraig

33

My picture is about a camp and a Traveller man saying Creeper, seidógs are after me. I have twenty three in my family. Some of them are in Dublin, Trim, America and England. My brother Martin is gone for eight years to America and is married to an American girl. He has three children. My sister had a baby girl last night, she has two children now. I wouldn't like to go back to living in a tent, because it was too poor. I'd like to have a job of being a cop when I grow up. If I was a seidóg I'd watch out for people breaking into houses and stealing and breaking into shops. My family would be happy if I was a seidóg. Settled people and Travellers are getting on well in Mohill and around towns.

Stephen,

CREEPER - CAT
SEIDÓGS - GUARDS

My brother Martin is gone for eight years to America and is married to an American girl. He has three children. My sister had a baby girl last night, she has two children now.

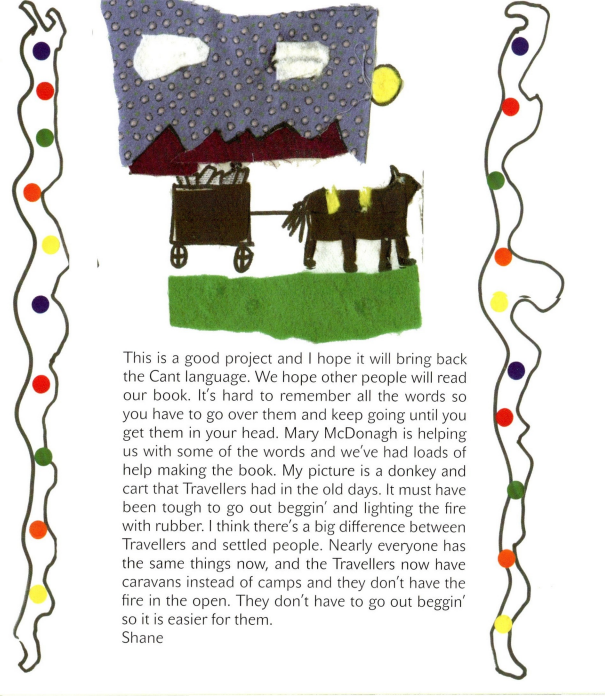

This is a good project and I hope it will bring back the Cant language. We hope other people will read our book. It's hard to remember all the words so you have to go over them and keep going until you get them in your head. Mary McDonagh is helping us with some of the words and we've had loads of help making the book. My picture is a donkey and cart that Travellers had in the old days. It must have been tough to go out beggin' and lighting the fire with rubber. I think there's a big difference between Travellers and settled people. Nearly everyone has the same things now, and the Travellers now have caravans instead of camps and they don't have the fire in the open. They don't have to go out beggin' so it is easier for them.

Shane

35

Travellers were the first people to start re-cycling. It was better to recycle in the old days instead of having bottles on the side of the roads or the fields. Travellers collected up as many bottles as they can and they brought them to the barman for money. Maybe they only got a penny or a halfpenny, but it was the only money they got. Nowadays Travellers recycle scrap.

Val

WHAT DID YOU DO WITH JAM JARS AND BOTTLES?

Well, long ago maybe the farmer would bring home half a dozen bottles of Guinness and he might throw them in the garden or under the hedge and Travellers would collect them and get a halfpenny each for them in any pub.

I hope that younger Travellers would find out what their Gran parents went

through in the old times. Times were hard for many people in the old days.

I hate school but I'd be very bored at home.

WHERE USED YOU BRING THEM?

We'd bring the jam jars to a shop in Annaduff because they used to make their own jam and you could bring the Guinness bottles to any pub. Or maybe you'd get someone coming round every three or four months and all you'd get for a lorry load was ten shillings. But ten shillings was money that time. And the horse hair was big that time too, from the tail and the mane and it was used to make mattresses.

37

WHAT COUNTIES DID YOU LIVE IN?

All of them, all 32 of them, we lived all over the world.

WAS THERE ANY CARS THAT TIME?

No, well Travellers didn't have cars them times. But the country people had them.

DID YOU LIVE IN A FIELD?

No, we lived on the side of the road.

DID YOU HAVE PETS?

No, we only had children.

DID YOU HAVE CHILDREN?

Well if I didn't have no children you'd have no mother.

WHAT DO YOU THINK WILL HAPPEN IN A FEW YEARS TIME TO TRAVELLERS?

In the future, I don't see any Travellers travelling except that they'd be going to funerals or weddings or going to things like that. There'll be no more camps for that day is gone and you're not allowed to stay on the side of the road now anyhow because it's too dangerous. The only way you'd get big groups of Travellers is at funerals because they do show an awful lot of respect. And then for weddings they're all open invitation so any one can go to them. That's when you get an awful lot of Travellers coming in. And I think now there'll be more change. There'll be bigger weddings, there'll be more getting married but they'll be a lot older from 18 up to 20s instead of younger. There'll be big change alright, but I think they might be all things for the better. But we'll still be Travellers no mat-ter what way you look at it. The Traveller's culture will never go. It will always be in the blood of the Traveller to be a Traveller

DID IT RAIN IN THE OLD DAYS?

It did, but the summers were longer and better, from April up 'til September. The weather is worser now.

.

I hope that younger Travellers would find out what their Gran parents went through in the old times. Times were hard for many people in the old days. My uncle had to stay at home from school because my Grandfather was sick and he'd do all the farming and planting the pota-toes. He went to school until he was 16 but didn't get a chance to go on. I hate school but I'd be very bored at home.

Niall

WHAT HAPPENED IF SOMEONE GOT SICK?

T'was the very rare Traveller got sick, they were reared up with the wind, the rain and it didn't affect them. They lived up 'til the nineties and hundreds after rearing twenty children on the side of the road. Me own mother is well mobilised and knows her pennies and her halfpennies. Don't take this the wrong way but Travellers would never put an old person into a home. An odd one might do it but they always try to keep the family together 'til they die. My mother's uncle was ninety five when he died.

HOW DID YOU GET THE COFFIN? ARE THE FUNERALS THE SAME?

They would be the same but maybe not as big, because you had to travel by horse and cart that time. Travellers always respected the dead, they'd feel guilty if they didn't go and show respect. It was the hearse that brought the coffin.

WAS THERE ANY CHRISTMAS THEM TIMES?

There was Christmas but not for the Travellers. There were no toys, computers or presents, you were lucky to have something to eat. It was only in the last 20 years Santy started coming to the Travellers. To be honest you mightn't even have a turkey. My mother might make a currant cake and that was her Christmas cake. All we had was whatever the farmer gave you. We used to call it a Christmas box.

DID YOU HAVE HALLOWEEN?

No, no trick or treating either. But one thing we did have was the Wren Boys going out singing and dancing and getting money off the people on St Stephens' Day. The Wren Boys were always there. The mummers is another name for it. That's right. The Travellers looked forward to that. They dressed up and all, maybe putting an old curtain round them, or putting their coat on inside out. They'd always put something on their face, maybe the straw or get a bit of coal and blacken their faces.

40

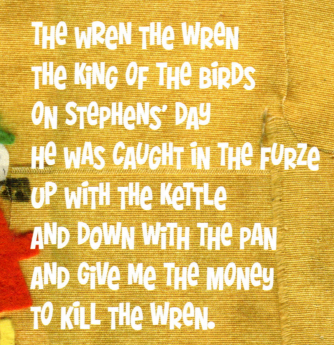

THE WREN THE WREN
THE KING OF THE BIRDS
ON STEPHENS' DAY
HE WAS CAUGHT IN THE FURZE
UP WITH THE KETTLE
AND DOWN WITH THE PAN
AND GIVE ME THE MONEY
TO KILL THE WREN.

The wren the   of the birds

On Stephens'.   i

up with the kettle and down with the pan

and give me the money to kill the wren.

THE WREN

SO YOU HAVE NINETEEN BROTHERS AND SISTERS?

Well, there's only eighteen of us living now and my own mother will be eighty soon.

MARY THAT'S UNUSUAL IN THE WORLD TODAY, BUT THERE IS ANOTHER FAMILY IN MOHILL WITH TWENTY CHILDREN?

Bernie and Mary Mc Donagh have twenty children, God bless them and Bernadette, Stephen and Darren and Val are in our workshop. The Reilly family had twenty in the family too but the parents were killed in a car accident a few years back.

T'was a very hard life that time with no schooling, you might make your communion on a Saturday and the following Sunday you made your confirmation. And that was it, when

you came to fourteen the Travellers would say, a big girl going to school, she should be out geigin' or getting married. That's why they got married so young.

HOW MANY CHILDREN DID YOU HAVE MARY?

I had 13 children but two of them were killed on the road on me. My gosson lived for nine months in a coma before he died he'd be twenty years old in July if he lived.

My picture shows a Traveller boy getting a beating. His father is hitting him with a sally rod because the boy did something bold. Parents nowadays can't hit their kids although they might threaten it. This is a good project because we are learning about different cultures, and a new language. We need to learn about other people so we won't discriminate because we don't understand them. We hope our book will teach people about Traveller language and culture.

Rowan

43

CURES

TRAVELLERS ARE VERY RELIGIOUS AREN'T THEY?

Travellers have a strong belief in Holy wells, and Knock and other holy pilgrimages. Travellers believe in cures too.

.

WHAT'S A CURE?

You might hear of someone who had the cure for the burn, or the cure for the headache, the cure for the back, and that. You have to believe in them and Traveller have a big belief in them.
My grandad has the cure of the sprain. He got a piece of string and tied it on my finger and said the prayer and it got better.
A lot of people now has the cure of the thrush, they blow their breath into the baby's neck and say three Hail Mary's and that'd be the cure of the thrush. There was a lot of cures and Travellers get them to this day. The mass might be dying out with some of them but not the cures. Like the seventh son of the seventh son and all that. They say that the cure can be passed on in the family. How they do that I don't know, but it must be in the blood. My granda got the cure of the shingles, he got the ointment and put it on his back and he got better.
The cure for the burns is the dripping of beef blessed and you put it in a little tub. The man out the Carrick road has it.

I believe in the cures of burns. Years ago when I was in baby infants I had a burn on my foot, and the doctor said there was nothing that would make it better, I got the cure of the burn for it, and i put it on my foot and a month later it was better.
Mary Bridget

IS THERE A CURE FOR WARTS?

There is a well in Longford in the old graveyard and you dip your finger in the holy well in the tree. It's a very powerful cure. You leave a little piece of string there, or a medal or something and you'll get the cure.

Is there a cure for warts?

There is a well in Longford in the old graveyard and you dip your finger in the holy well in the tree. It's a very powerful cure. You leave a little piece of string there, or a medal or something and you'll get the cure.

GLOSSARY OF CANT WORDS

chimógs sticks
lúbán tent
lí bed
nobera turf
goyas children
chera fire
geigin begging
cénas houses
lurp flour
weed tea
grucaire sugar
gairead money
chercs clothes
dora bread
guillimíns shoes

skoi water
alamach milk
salked sold
nucs pennies
gleoch man
fé meat
cob cabbage
cullens spuds
grag town
missel go/get
beoirs women
steamers cigs
súbla boy
lakín girl
rúmógs eggs

Súbla
Lakín
Gleoch
Beoir
Goyas
Séideog

Consra
Creper
Múóg
Corras
Claudóg
Laprog
Blanóg
Bleater

Cant?

HOW WE MADE THIS BOOK

We began at the beginning; we met the crew, Orla and the two Marys. We were then given a copy of the previous book entitled, Can't Lose Cant. So we had a framework on which we could create our own book. We were then taught the meanings of some fifty words in the language. We were then instructed to make pictures out of various disused materials. In our pictures we were supposed to immortalise and visualise aspects of a Traveller's way of life. There were many colourful ideas and general enthusiasm for this strange and alien language. Once all our pictures were complete, we were then commissioned the task of titling our work of reference. Once the title was decided we were then split into groups and commissioned different tasks all involved in the editing or composing the content, book's cover, appendix, introduction etc. So from there I suppose it's to the publishing house, and I hope it goes well. Many sincere thanks and gratitude to all those involved.

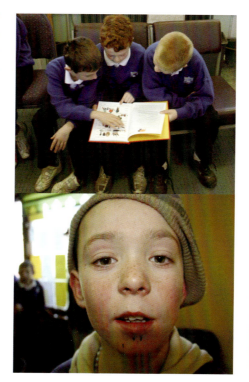

WE HOPE YOU ENJOY IT!

Other Titles by Kids...

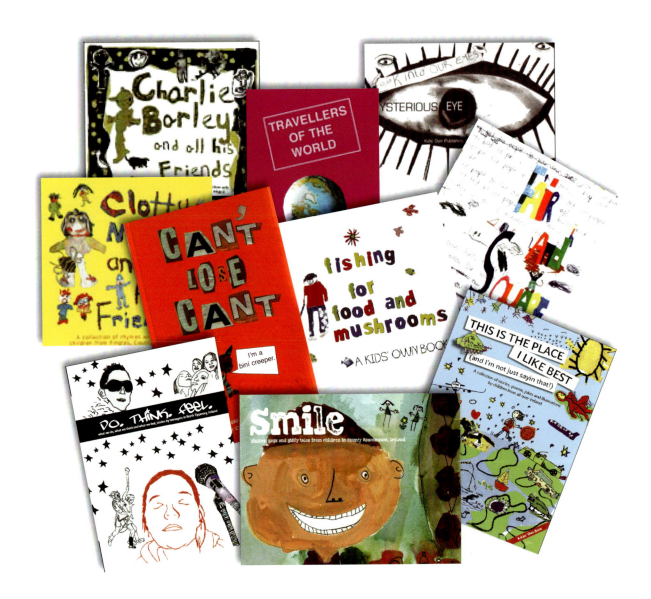

KIDS' OWN PUBLISHING PARTNERSHIP, CARRIGEENS, BALLINFUL, SLIGO • T: 00353 71 912 4945 • e: INFO@KIDSOWN.ie • W: HTTP://KIDSOWN.ie